Poems To Help Your
Christian Walk

BRIAN TAYLOR

WESTBOW
PRESS®
A DIVISION OF THOMAS NELSON
& ZONDERVAN

WestBow Press books may be ordered through booksellers or by contacting:

WestBow Press
A Division of Thomas Nelson & Zondervan
1663 Liberty Drive
Bloomington, IN 47403
www.westbowpress.com
844-714-3454

ISBN: 978-1-6642-3323-2 (sc)
ISBN: 978-1-6642-3325-6 (hc)
ISBN: 978-1-6642-3324-9 (e)

Library of Congress Control Number: 2021908757

Print information available on the last page.

WestBow Press rev. date: 5/11/2021

Acknowledgment

Poems were inspired by daily reading the
New King James Version Bible

Contents

Poems by Brian Taylor

Difficulties and challenges will arrive at some point in our lives. When I went through a difficult bout with Covid, my dependency upon the Lord increased. My time spent in the Biblical scriptures also increased. The poems that I wrote were Divinely inspired and expressed my need for the help of my Savior Jesus Christ. I hope these poems can help build your relationship with Jesus Christ also.

"Jesus Christ is the same yesterday, today, and forever"-Hebrews 13:8

Encouragement

Be courageous when difficulties arise
Taking on battles without fear
Supernatural strength will come upon you
Your victory is near

Relationship With Christ

We honor Jesus our Lord
When we bow down before Him as King of Kings
Forgive us Lord when we come to You only to be gratified
Enter His presence with Thanksgiving and singing

Always Pray

God has an answer for every prayer
His answers lead to our well-being
Keep your spirit free of sin and complaining
Come to the Lord expecting and rejoicing

Don't Complain

Christians are at their best
Coming to the Lord being humble
The Lord Almighty doesn't want us
To have spirits that mumble and grumble

Newness In Christ

God's timing is everything
Trust Him that He'll do what He said He'd do
God always keeps His promises
He makes all things new

The Light

The Light shines in my life
Jesus Christ is the Light
The Light gives me strength
Jesus Christ brings me peace during the day and at night

Don't Blame God

Let us not blame God
When life throws us curve balls
By not living in the peace of the Lord
You'll slam against many walls

Wait

Wait upon the Lord
Keep his promises in your heart
Always show your love for Him
Don't let fear tear you apart

Alive In Christ

I'm alive in Christ
He gives me a reason to live
Christ always demonstrates His love
He is right there ready to forgive

The Power of God

Satan lies to you
Don't give Him any power
Your faith needs to be in The Lord
The name of the Lord is a strong tower

Holiness

Holiness is still essential in Christianity
Being in awe of the Lord's sovereignty
Let's always show The Lord reverence
And not despise Biblical prophecy

Adoration

Don't take God's name in vain
Your mouth needs to edify the Lord
The Lord delights in communicating with Believers
The Lord is to be adored

Secure In the Lord

Help me Lord in my life
Give me supernatural strength I don't possess
Reveal your plans as I pray
Let me be secure in your eternal rest

Trinity

The Holy Spirit will always reveal truth
When you receive Jesus Christ as Lord
The Father, Son, and Holy Spirit
Work together in one accord

What Is Mine

My faith is in God's Word
God's Word is divine
Jesus Christ is my Lord
His joy and peace are mine

Majesty

We worship the King of Kings
Jesus Christ is our King
He will rule righteously in the near future
What glorious majesty Jesus Christ will bring

Repentance Of Sin

When you repent of your sin
You leave it for good
Sin destroys communication with God
It will ruin your livelihood

Making A Decision

Seek Jesus Christ when you make a decision
Do what He tells you to do
You will appreciate your results
Jesus Christ is always faithful and true

Healing

Jesus Christ is our healer
No healing occurs outside of Him
Pray and believe for your healing
Even if the doctor's news is grim

The Church

Christ's love for His church
Will always be protected
The church is a special place
That Christ hasn't rejected

Jerusalem

Jerusalem needs daily prayers
Rogue nations want to attack her
Pray for Jerusalem's protection
Jesus Christ will rule Jerusalem for sure

Prophecy

Preachers who preach prophecy
Are obeying the Lord
Prophecy is one-fourth of the Bible
Prophecy in the pulpit shouldn't be ignored

Jesus' Return

Jesus Christ is coming soon
All the signs of His Coming are here
Prepare your hearts to meet Christ the Lord
The Biblical Christian doesn't need to fear

Victory In Jesus

You can be strong in the Lord
When trials come your way
Step out and walk in victory
Time spent with Jesus is great everyday

Strength In the Lord

It is time to wake up
The Coming of the Lord Jesus Christ isn't too far off
Be strengthened by the power of His might
Don't grow weary or soft

The Cross

What is your Cross to bear?
Jesus Christ won't let you bear it alone
Give your all to Jesus
His Blood bought sacrifice atones

God's Truth

No matter what Satan throws at you
The truth of God's Word stands
Say the scriptures aloud all the time
You are in the Lord's Hands

The Millennium

Jesus Christ will reign on Earth
For one thousand years
What an awesome time this will be
Jesus Christ will wipe away all your tears

God Is On My Mind

Think about what pleases the Lord
Let the Lord guide your thinking
Stay focused on Biblical truths
So your mind won't go sinking

Our Provider

God provides everything you have
Thank Him for what He's given you
Appreciate God as your provider
God is faithful and true

The Scriptures

Follow the scriptures
They are just as true today
The scriptures speak to your hearts
The Bible is here to stay

Feelings Versus Healings

Let the spirit of God
Overrule your feelings
No matter what you see
Be expectant of your healings

Storms

Trust the Lord in your storm
The storm may be violent
Talk to God out loud about your storm
Don't stay silent

God's Wisdom Versus the Flesh

Put no confidence in the flesh
You will more often fail
If you don't depend on God's wisdom
When you have problems you will probably fail

God Is Near

The Lord's tender voice
Can be heard if you have ears to hear
You need to keep the Lord's Word in your heart
The Lord is always near

God and Your Money

God speaks plenty about money
Money should be used with wisdom
Give the Lord the first ten percent
You will experience more Godly freedom

Pleasing God

God calls us to be holy
It's how we please Him
We take on more of God's character traits
Your life will not look so dim

Awareness Of God

Be aware of the Lord
The Lord is everywhere
Everything was made by Him
Treat everything He's made with proper care

God Forgives

There are consequences to sin
When you don't repent
Go to Jesus Christ and ask for forgiveness
This is why Jesus Christ was sent

Biblical Truth

You cannot eliminate Biblical truths
That last for all eternity
People who reject what's in the Bible
Is a shameful pity

Increase In God

Love the Lord God with all your heart
Your trust will increase
Our Lord God desires this personal relationship
He must increase while I must decrease

Joy

Joy comes from the Lord
It's ruminating from your heart
Joy radiates your personality
Joy in the morning gives you a good head start

Peace In Christ

Love Christ every moment of the day
Keep Him focused on your mind
Call out to Jesus regularly
He will be the best peace you'll ever find

Your Future In God

God knows where you're going
He is guiding your path
God is planning a great life for eternity
To save you from wrath

Israel

Israel will always be loved by the Lord
Israel is the "Apple of His Eye"
The Lord has chastened and loved Israel
The state of Israel will live and never die

Glory In the Lord

Glorifying our Lord Jesus
Is why the Lord has you living
Loving others and expressing joy
And when you're angry you're always forgiving

I'm Healed

Your healing has arrived
You thanked God for the outcome
You shout victory in Jesus' Name
Sing joyfully to the Lord and beat that drum!

Follow the Light

God gives us light
His light will bring you His peace
Walk in His light each day
And your depression and darkness will cease

Focus On the Lord

Pray for what the Lord wants
God's agenda is what Believers should desire
God is pleased when we focus on His plans
Our world needs to see some Holy fire

Being A Servant

Look for ways to serve someone
Jesus Christ was always serving others
Who do you begin to serve?
Begin serving mother, father, sisters, and brothers

Be Thankful

Give thanks unto the Lord
Make this a regular routine
You will have more joy in your life
You'll experience more blessings you've ever seen

Have Faith and Don't Grumble

Don't indict God
God always has a purpose
If you're always complaining to God
There'll be something valuable you'll miss

Jesus, the Lord of Israel

Blessed be the Lord God of Israel
Everyone will say this aloud someday
Jesus Christ will rule Israel
The Heavenly ruler of Israel is The Way

My Attitude Towards God

God is up to something
I need to trust and obey
Be thankful and show love
Everyday can be a good day

The Door

Look for The Door
Don't be blind to where it is
Jesus Christ is The Door
All blessings in life are His

A Thought About Paul

Our suffering
Doesn't compare to the Apostle Paul
He was strengthened by the Lord
Paul answered the Lord's call

God's Word

The truth of God's Word
Will always prevail
Hold onto the truth with your life
God's Word will never fail

The Armor of God

Don't let Satan destroy you
Your battle belongs to the Lord
The Lord handles these battles perfectly
Christian soldiers need to activate their heavenly swords

God's Help

Revive us Lord
We come to You with repentant hearts
The Lord will help you
Overcome the Devil's fiery darts

See What God Sees

The Will of God
Prevails no matter what you believe
The Lord God Almighty
Can do more than what you can conceive

Paying the Price

A price has been paid on your life
Jesus Christ died on the Cross for you
His efficacious blood gives you life
Your life becomes brand new

Jesus Has Saved You

Be an investor in the Lord's kingdom
Souls need to be saved
Jesus Christ came to save people who are sick
He also came to save the depraved

God's Love Fills You

Love God with a kind spirit
Let God's love flow all over you
Embrace His love with your whole being
Letting God's love fill you will keep you from feeling blue

Needing the Lord

I need the Lord
More than I need my daily comforts
I can't survive without the Lord
I want to live within the Lord's heavenly courts

The End Times

The End Times are here
Jesus Christ is returning soon
All the signs have been fulfilled
He might return this afternoon

Treat God Right

If you want more grace and peace
More knowledge of God's love is needed
Study the Bible and increase your prayer time
The way you treat God is the way you'll be treated

The Image of God

Bear the image of the Lord God
Surrender the image of Adam
The image of God represents true abundant life
Go through Jesus Christ who's the lion and the lamb

Faith In God

Without faith it's impossible to please God
Faith without works is dead
Do what God tells you to do
It's vital to do what God has said

Being In Heaven

Jesus Christ spoke a lot about Heaven
It's a really special place
Jesus was very specific of what Heaven is like
In Heaven, we will see Jesus's face

Eternity With Christ

The Lord welcomes anyone to Heaven
If you accept Jesus Christ in your heart
Live to win souls for eternity
How great thou art!

The Brightest Light

What is the brightest light
That radiates glory
The brightest light is Jesus Christ
Jesus Christ is the greatest everlasting story

Don't Divide Israel

Jerusalem is very special to our Lord
All of Jerusalem belongs to Israel
Enemies of our Lord want Israel divided
Dividing Israel will ultimately fail

A Person's Heart

A servant's heart
Is what the Lord is looking for
The Lord looks into each person's heart
What's in a person's heart is your true core

Cry out To God

Cry unto the Lord
When you've grived the Holy Spirit
Repent and pour your heart in prayer
So you don't fall in a bottomless pit

The Apple Of His Eye

Stand up for Israel
Pray for America's closest ally
Don't support the Boycott Divestment Sanctions
Israel is the "Apple of His Eye"

Connection and Protection

Worship the Lord with your whole heart
Seeking the Lord making a connection
Being strengthened by the Holy Spirit each day
You will experience the Lord's protection

Our Jewish Friends

Pray for our Jewish friends
Anti-Semitism has been on the rise
Christians need to speak out against Jewish persecution
Don't support Anti-Semitic lies

God's Guidance

Be bold in your faith
Trust that God is protecting you
Share the love of Jesus Christ when opportunity comes
God will guide you in what to do

The Breath Of God

Every breath is a gift from the Lord
The air we breathe is life to us
Give thanks to God for every breath
It is the Lord our God we must trust

Don't Walk In Darkness

Don't let darkness settle over your city
Darkness will destroy the longer it stays
Jesus Christ can take away that darkness
Call on the light of the Ancient of Days

God's Children

Remember the days of your Creator
When the Lord came through for you
The Lord loves to bless His children
He has blessed the Gentile and Jew

Seek the Lord"

You can enjoy the kingdom now
Seeking the Lord in everything
Enjoy serving the Lord in whatever you do
When you do this your heart will sing

The Heavenly Voice

Jesus Christ will return to Earth
Lift up your heart and rejoice
The Lord's perfect peace will be coming
Be ready to hear His Heavenly voice

A Troubled Heart

If your heart is troubled
Immediately go to the Lord in prayer
You will be settled in your spirit
You will be strengthened by the Lord's care

Pray Continuously

The Lord needs to be everything in your life
Depend on the Lord 24 hours a day
Live to enjoy being in the Lord's presence
Throughout each day pray, pray, pray!

God's Welcoming

I can't wait till I get to Heaven
I will finally meet my Lord
His Pearly Gates will be wide open
With a great big sign to all Believers, "Welcome Aboard"

God Knows

You've shared with me
What's on your troubled heart
Now pray to the Lord for guidance
He'll show you where you need to start

God Can Handle It

Life is a challenge
We jump through hurdles on a daily basis
Start the day off with prayer
And God will handle all your cases

God's Deliverance

The fear in my life
Is slowly going away
If I come across any uncertain situation
All I need to do is relax and pray

Lord You are guiding me
Wherever I may go
I will always be protected
He will deliver me from every foe

Being With God

I have the time to think about
What living with the spirit of God is like
The experience is truly amazing
I can compare it to a never ending nature hike

Forgiveness and Cleansing

Jesus, I ask for Your forgiveness
Enter my life today
My spirit needs cleansing
And may all the oppressive spirits inside me be cast away

My Hero

I want to share who my hero is
He brought me out of the dark
His name is Jesus Christ our Lord and Savior
Thank You Jesus for giving my life that desperately needed a spark

Take A Look

It is time to take a look
At where my life is heading
Have I been a faithful servant and giver to You Lord?
Or have I been so preoccupied with just getting

God Will Show You

The love that Jesus Christ has for me
Is so awesome, He guides me everyday
If I ever get in trouble and need help
Jesus will surely show me the way

Praising God

There is joy amongst Christians
They are praising the Lord through worship and song
Miracles are being performed as Believers pray at the altars
Jesus Christ has the power to heal and you won't go wrong

Give It To God

I look into your eyes
Tears of sadness are flowing down very slowly
You need to share what's inside your heart
Give whatever is binding you over to Jesus who's pure and holy

God Redeems

There is joy in my heart
Jesus and I are together, not apart
We make a great team
It's through You Lord that I have been redeemed

Problems

Is there a problem in your life?
That just doesn't seem to go away
God knows what you're struggling with
He is there to help you everyday

Trust God

Spend a quiet hour
Focusing on the Lord's awesome power
God loves each one of us
He is who we need to trust

True Peace

Who is able to obtain peace?
A wary soul wants to know
My heart is at ease
The Lord has conquered every foe

True peace in life
Isn't available without Jesus Christ
There will be misery and strife in this world
But the Lord is watching us with His Heavenly eyes

Peace is only possible
If you understand God's Word
The Lord will do the impossible
Accept in your heart what Christ has offered

A gift that has been given to you
Needs to be fully cultivated
If you develop the gift of the Lord's peace
The Holy Spirit will be elated

Printed in the United States
by Baker & Taylor Publisher Services